Empowerment of Rural Women Entrepreneurs in Agricultural Sector: A Study in Erode District of Tamil Nadu

Dr.K.M. Deepa

Published by

Empowerment of Rural Women Entrepreneurs in Agricultural Sector: A Study in Erode District of Tamil Nadu

ISBN 978-93-87862-03-6

Author

Dr.K.M. Deepa

Bonfring

309, 2nd Floor,

5th Street Extension, Gandhipuram,

Coimbatore-641 012.

Tamilnadu, India.

E-mail: info@bonfring.org

Website: www.bonfring.org

Phone: 0422 4213231

Preface

Empowerment strategies nowadays have emerged as a unique Indian response to the challenge of gender equity and development. For women empowerment, it is essential to provide them access to information, knowledge, resources and power to make decisions. Empowering women at all sphere of life plays a vital role and is crucial in sustainable development of the nation. The analysis of conditions leading to their powerlessness, need implementation of suitable managerial skill trainings, motivation to decision-making with persistence for accomplishing basic objectives will lead those empowered women in agriculture. The process of empowerment will not only be able to improve their skills and access to productive resources, but also succeed in enhancing quality, dignity and work in the society status.

The effect of empowerment of women creates a powerful influence on the norms, values and finally the laws that govern these communities. They, thus, move away from being ineffective subordinate in the decision making with improvement in managing their lives. Empowerment includes cognitive and psychological elements, such as a women's understanding of her condition of subordination and the causes of such conditions. This requires an understanding the self and the cultural and social expectations, which may be activated by education. Women's empowerment is a socio-political concept that involves cognitive, psychological, economic and political dimensions. The reasons for empowerment often arise when an individual or group of individuals are unable or prevented from actualizing their potentials due to barriers created by individuals or other people within the environment.

This book is a miniature attempt to explore the factors influencing the women entrepreneurs' entre into the agricultural sector, problems faced by rural women entrepreneurs in agricultural sector, various schemes and institutions of women entrepreneurs in agricultural sector and their awareness level, satisfaction level of women entrepreneurs in agricultural sector. It is impossible to write a book without the help and contributions of many other people. I owe a large debt to all my teachers and my family members. I express my sincere thanks to Bonfring Publication for having undertaken this assignment and the successful publication of my work.

Above all, I am grateful to God for his blessing and grace.

Dr.K.M. Deepa

<table>
<tr><td>Chapter</td><td>Contents</td><td>Page No</td></tr>
</table>

CHAPTER I

INTRODUCTION AND DESIGN OF THE STUDY

1.1. Introduction

Mahatma Gandhi Says, "Woman is the companion of man, gifted with equal mental capacities. She has the right to participate in minutest details and liberty as he. She is entitled to a supreme place in her own sphere of activity as man is in his. Man and woman are equal in status but are not identical. They are peerless pair being complementary to one another: each helps the other, so that without the one. the existence of the other cannot be conceived, and therefore, it follows as a necessary corollary from these facts that anything that will impair the status of either of them will involve the equal ruin of both." Due to changing environment, changing technology, improved social and economic conditions, and man's income is not sufficient to the family. Women also need to work and earn income. Thus women resources are also to be exploited. Women need not seek job from others but also she can create one for herself. Indian Government encourages women to go for self employment. By becoming an entrepreneur, woman can be self employed and provide employment to others also.

Women entrepreneurs play an important role in all countries, especially in developing countries like India. The fifth round of National Sample Survey Organization (NSSO) in March 20002 defined "women entrepreneur as "an owned and controlled by women having a minimum financial investment of 51% of the capital and giving at least 51% of the employment generated in the enterprise to women". However, this definition is subject to criticism mainly on the condition of employing more than 50% women workers employed in the enterprises and owned and run by women. In a nutshell, women entrepreneurs are those women who think of a business enterprise, initiate it, organize and combine the factors of production, operate the enterprise and undertake risks and handle economic uncertainty included in running a business enterprise.

The basic objective of women entrepreneurs is the creation of employment opportunities. With the development of women entrepreneurs, there can be dispersal of industries in the country. Women entrepreneurs facilitate a more equitable distribution of the national income and they ensure the achievement of technical improvements. Since the labourers do not have any disturbance in their local and social habits and customs, women entrepreneurs lead to progressive improvement in productivity.

Swaminathan, the famous agricultural scientist describes that it was woman who first domesticated crop plants and thereby initiated the art and science of farming. While men went out hunting in search of food, women started gathering seeds from the native flora and began cultivating those of interest from the point of view of food, feed, fodder, fibre and fuel. Women have played and continue to play a key role in the conservation of basic life support systems such as land, water, flora and fauna. They have protected the health of the soil through organic recycling and promoted crop security through the maintenance of varietal diversity and genetic resistance.

That women play a significant and crucial role in agricultural development and allied fields including in the main crop production, livestock production, horticulture, post harvest operations, agro/social forestry, fisheries, etc. The nature and extent of women's involvement in agriculture, no doubt, varies greatly from region to region. Even within a region, their involvement varies widely among different ecological sub-zones, farming systems, castes, classes and stages in the family cycle. But regardless of these variations, there is hardly any activity in agricultural production, except ploughing in which women are not actively involved. Studies on women in agriculture conducted in India and other developing and under developed countries all point to the conclusion that women contribute far more to agricultural production than has generally been acknowledged. Recognition of their crucial role in agriculture should not obscure the fact that farm women continue to be concerned with their primary functions as wives, mothers and homemakers.

Despite their importance to agricultural production, women face severe handicaps. They are in fact, the largest group of landless labourers with little real security in case of break-up of the family owing to death or divorce; inheritance laws and customs discriminate against them land reform and settlement programmes usually give sole title and hence the security needed for obtaining production credits to the husband. Agricultural development programmes are usually planned by men and aimed at men. Mechanization, for example alleviates the burden of tasks that are traditionally men's responsibility, leaving women's burdens unrelieved or even increased.

It may not be out of place to mention here that considering their dual responsibilities within and outside the home, it would be in the fitness of things that more and more in the village training is organized for rural farm women to suit their convenience with due realization that institutional training is important in its own place. In order that farm women get a fair deal at the hands of change agents, one of the remedial measures that needs to be undertaken is to induct a sizeable number of well trained women personnel in training and extension programmes of agricultural development agencies at all levels and more so at the grass-root level. Around the world, there are at least 1.6 billion women who live in rural areas and depend on agriculture for their livelihoods – more than a quarter of the total world population. Women farmers produce more than half of all the food that is grown in the world, specifically, up to 80 percent in Africa and 60 percent in Asia.

Research has shown that when women increase their incomes and have access to more resources, they invest their money in their children's nutrition, education and health care, creating a multiplier effect that strengthens families and communities over time. Yet, despite the benefits for both agricultural productivity and poverty reduction, many development programs and services do not adequately invest in women's agricultural productivity. Women receive only about five percent of all agricultural extension resources ii and own only an estimated two percent of all titled land worldwide.

Given women and men's different roles and access to resources, it is essential that agricultural projects take gender differences into account. Too often, gender is equated with women, but gender is about women and men. Gender refers to the different roles, resources, rights, opportunities and responsibilities of women and men in a society. Decades of research and experience have shown that these differences between women and men are profound in the developing world. Furthermore, women and men face differing constraints and opportunities - especially in terms of their needs for, and access to, services and programs. Because of historic and cultural barriers, without a focus on gender, women's needs are most often left out.

1.2.   Early Concept of Entrepreneurship

In 1951 census, the approach was income based whereas the 1961 census was based on work in terms of time or labour force as per recommendation of ILO (International Labour Organization). Following the adoption of work approach in 1961 census, the classification of population was done into two categories –workers and non workers. A person was treated as worker if he or she devoted more than one hour a day for regular work for a larger part of the working season or if he or she was employed during any of the fifteen days preceding the visiting day of enumeration to the household.

In 1971 census also, the population was divided into two broad streams of main activity as workers and non workers. If a person had participated in any economic activity on any single day during the reference period (one week to the date of enumeration) was treated as main worker and the rest were treated as nonworking even if they were engaged in same economic activity partly or wholly during the year excluding the reference period. The non workers were those who had not worked at all during the reference year. In other words, the strength of non workers could be arrived at by subtracting the total strength of main and marginal workers from the total population.

While formulating the economic aspect for 1981 census, a tracheotomy of persons into mutually exclusive groups of main workers, marginal workers and non workers was introduced. Finally, as 1991 census based on the discussions in the data user conference, it was decided unanimously to follow the concepts and definitions used in 1981 census including the reference period of one year for both regular and seasonal activities.

1.3. Changing Role of Women

The decades after independence have seen tremendous changes in the status and the position of the women in Indian society. The constitution has laid down as a fundamental right – the equality of the sexes. It would not be an exaggeration to say that the recent changes in the status of women in India is nota sign of progress, but it is really a recapturing of the position that was held by women in Vedic period. Jayapalan in his book on women studies in 2000 describes the changing roles as follows:

1.3.1. Social Role

Literary and historical research has now established beyond doubt that the women held a position of equality with men during the Vedic period. There was a great change in the role of women after 300 B. C. During this period, son was valued more than daughter. Many young women renounced their homes and joined the Buddhistic and Jain monasteries. It was also presumed that one of the reasons for practice of early marriage of girls was to prevent them from entering monastic life. Girls were married off soon after puberty. Marriage was an irrevocable union for a woman. The wave of reformist movement in nineteenth century brought the changing role of women in the social field. Finally it led to the great emancipation of the Indian women in the twentieth century. There was a change in the outlook in society. Many legislative measures were brought about for the protection of women. The urgency of women's education was felt and thus facilities for the same were made. Many women leaders created a kind of political awareness among women which led to a great change in their role. Women even began to fight against the social evils during this period.

1.3.2. Economic Role

Rural women have always been working in the fields and farms from time immemorial. They have worked because that was way of life. Similarly women have been working to help their husbands in cottage industries. They have been working and they now continue to work. Work in the lives of majority of women is not a matter of self equity. Changing economic roles and responsibilities of women, particularly among the poor, make employment/work a matter of economic survival. Male unemployment or male low earnings resulting due to wage labour and high rates of urbanization have also meant an increase in the number of married women workers. Low male wages often impose double responsibilities on married women who need to substitute the family income through additional home production and work outside the home. Women's contribution to household income provides the means to meet basic survival needs such as food, clothing and shelter. Ultimately, women's contribution makes possible improvements in the health and nutritional status of 1household members. In the census, "married women' are often classified as "housewives", weighing the importance of economic contribution they make to the household. The actual number of economically active married women is much larger than aggregate level data would indicate.

The great change, however took place when the machines were introduced. Women were employed in factories. In 1901 as many as 6, 38,000 women worked in factories, mines and plantations, forming 14.5 percent of the total working force. There was spectacular increase in the employment of middle class women who were working in secretarial or administrative capacities. More women were now working as stenographers, clerks, telephone operators and receptionists; In the educational field also about 15 percents of the teachers at primary and secondary levels were women. Women's participation in all spheres highlights their changing role and the emerging pattern points towards equality of sex.

1.4. Economic Contribution of Women

It has been well accepted that women play an important role in economic welfare of the family. It is generally felt that the role of women in traditional societies is just confined to the household management based on traditional values, attitudes and customs. In fact, the family culture in the context of which early socialization takes place is a very important factor which later on induces or prohibits women's participation in economic activities of the family.

The emergence of women on the economic scene as entrepreneurs is a significant development in the emancipation of women and securing for them a place in the society, which they have all along deserved. The association of women with economic enterprises would provide a healing touch in promoting peace and amity in the strife ridden world of today. Legally and constitutionally, woman in India enjoy a unique status of equality with men. They are equal citizens expected to enjoy all the rights and privileges conferred upon all the people. They are entitled to same fundamental rights as Women entering business is comparatively recent phenomenon. By and they had confined to petty business and tiny cottage industries.

The emergence of women on the economic scene as entrepreneurs is a significant development in the emancipation of women and securing for them a place in the society, which they have all along deserved. The association of women with economic enterprises would provide a healing touch in promoting peace and amity in the strife ridden world of today. Legally and constitutionally, woman in India enjoy a unique status of equality with men. They are equal citizens expected to enjoy all the rights and privileges conferred upon all the people. They are entitled to same fundamental rights as are guaranteed to men. This provision has enabled the government to make special provision for women, particularly in the field of labour legislations like Factories Act, Maternity Benefit Act, etc. Indian women have played an outstanding role in the freedom struggle and contributed a great deal to the Indian cultural heritage. It is now extremely significant to see that they are not lagging behind in the process of economic growth.

1.4.1. *Women in Agriculture*

Women play an indispensable role in farming and in improving the quality of life in rural areas. However, their contributions often remain concealed due to some social barriers and gender bias. Even government programmes often fail to focus on women in agriculture. This undermines the potential benefits from programmes, especially those related to food production, household income improvements, nutrition, literacy, poverty alleviation and population control. Equitable access for rural women to educational facilities would certainly improve their performance and liberate them from their marginalized status in the society. Other areas where women's potential could be effectively harnessed are agricultural extension, farming systems development, land reform and rural welfare. Landmark improvements have been recorded in such cases as the extension of institutional credit and domestic water supplies where women's potential have been consciously tapped. Socio-economic goals of productivity, equity and environment stability are closely woven around the agriculture sector policies and new dimensions in programmes implemented are already emerging as new values. Regardless of the level of development achieved by the respective economies, women play a pivotal role in agriculture and in rural development in most countries of the Asia-Pacific Region. Asia-Pacific region had witnessed spectacular development in crop yields which even surpassed the population growth rate in the past decade. However, pockets of hunger remain when landless or small farm rural population lack economic access to food because of a lack of remunerative non-farm employment in rural areas, where 80% of Asia-Pacific's 400 million poor live. It has also been suggested that with the acceleration of crop-diversification programmes and the transformation of agriculture to commercial production levels, women's lot had been even further worsened by the addition of new burdens which they have to shoulder in order to realize profits in farm operations.

Rural women who are obliged to attend to all the household chores, children's welfare, nutrition and family cohesion along with farm work, are desperately driven to adopt a survival strategy to save the family food security from total collapse. Rural poverty has increased in the region particularly for farmers as priority has been accorded to the industrial and service sectors: this is both the cause and an effect of rural-urban migration leading to the "feminisation of farming". Thus the numbers and the proportion of rural women among the absolutely poor and destitute, currently around 60%, is expected to increase to 65 to 70% by the year 2000. In spite of social, political and economic constraints, women farmers have proved extremely resourceful and hardworking in their attempt to ensure household food security. Social constraints place barriers around their access to scientific and technological information.

After some decades of development, global problems and issues concerning environment, women in development, and poverty have reappeared. All these have emerged in rural communities and threatening their sustainability. Rural communities with norms developed for managing resources are important for the stability of community life. Gender-oriented rural development programmes which focus on role of women to guarantee the stability of life provide a sound basis for integrated development of the quality of life. In progressive economies like Japan, rural women have shown anxieties over several concerns affecting their livelihood. Some of the priority items include measures for success in agricultural enterprises, expansion of periodic farming resulting in reduced holidays, the need to reduce agricultural work, changes in awareness of rural societies and reduction in the work connected with caring for elderly people. In order to redress these problems, five tasks have been identified for promotion which will result in making rural living more pleasant and comfortable.

These tasks include:

i. Creating awareness of changes and measures pursued to change the status of women by their active participation in agricultural and fisheries cooperatives;

ii. Improving working conditions and environment;

iii. Appreciating the positive aspects of living in rural areas and creating a conducive environment which will contribute towards better rural life;

iv. Acquiring skills to diversify areas of involvement by women supporting women in entrepreneurial roles; and

v. Adopt a structured approach to execute the vision to improve rural conditions.

1.5. Statement of the Problem

These are several constraints faced by women entrepreneurs for entrepreneurial development in agricultural sector.

The problems faced by women in agriculture

1. What are the all factors influencing the women entrepreneurs in agricultural sectors?
2. What are all the problems faced by the women agricultural entrepreneurs?
3. To explain the schemes and institutions of agricultural women entrepreneurs and their level of awareness and schemes about the rural women agricultural entrepreneurs?
4. What are the satisfaction level of women entrepreneurs in agricultural sectors?

1.6. Review of the Literature

Entrepreneurship development in small-scale industry is a subject of pre dominant moral code of governance in all developing countries. Small enterprises are large in number and more are their participants: large number of entrepreneurs and employees. In this era of democracy, economic growth and development is determined by dynamic entrepreneurial resources present in a nation. A large number of studies have been conducted in this regard by various experts in this field. Multifarious criteria are used to determine factors responsible for entrepreneurial motivation, competitive strategies, performance and so on. A brief review of the important studies in this area is presented here. There is a vast body of literature linked with role of rural women in agriculture and its allied fields, but here we mention only recent work being done on the topic.

Panel .V[1] (2010) pointed out that women's work, in distinction to that of men's, encompasses paid activities but also many unpaid tasks that are critical for the survival of the household. The latter, unpaid work, includes subsistence production and unpaid family wok; gathering of free goods from common lands such as fruits, medicinal herbs, water and fuel wood; daily household maintenance, cooking and sanitation; and taking care of the ill, elderly, and children. Hence the world of women's work can only be understood when both paid and unpaid work is taken into account. Despite policy measures and programs that have been put in place to directly target the disadvantages women face in the world of work, outcomes show that much remains to be accomplished. in a world scale, the number of women of working age that participate in labour markets lags behind that of men. Unemployment rates among women, at the global level are higher; vulnerable work (family work and self-employment-which do provide social protection or benefits) is more prevalent among women; women comprise higher numbers- in most instances- of informal workers; and to add fuel to fire, when paid and unpaid work are accounted for, women work longer hours but receive lower pay than men.

Sunita Kishor and Kamla Gupta[2] (2009) in their study stated that over the past decade, gender equality and women's empowerment have been explicitly recognized as key not only to the health of nations, but also to social and economic development. India's National Population Policy 2000 has empowering women for health and nutrition as one of its crosscutting strategic themes. Additionally, the promotion of gender equality and empowering of women is one of the eight Millennium Development Goals (MDG) to which India is a signatory. The pairing of the two concepts of women's empowerment and gender equality into one MDG implicitly recognizes that gender equality and gender equality into one MDG implicitly recognizes that gender equality and women's empowerment are two sides of the same coin: progress toward gender equality requires women's empowerment and women's empowerment requires increases in gender equality as shown.

Santosh Kumar[3] (2005) in his study "Status of women in India during the are of globalzation" explained that in India the slogans of feminism and gender equality are still distant dreams as the issues of women in our country are neglected. After more than five decades of planned economic development, it is ironical that we are still trying to tackle, the

---

[1] Panel.V (2010), "Women's Economic Empowerment: The Most Vulnerable Groups", Development of rural women entrepreneurship,vol.1, pp 54-59.

[2] Sunitha Kishor and Kamala Gupta (2009), "Gender equality and women's empowerment in India", National Family Health Survey (NFHS-3).

[3] Santhosh Kumar (2005)," Status of Women in India during the Era Globalisation", Third concept, pp.33-35

basic need of a minimum standard of living such as drinking water, shelter, sanitation and employment. Women form almost half of the population in India. Yet their status in economic, political or in social life leaves much to be desired. This paper examines how the forces of globalization are degrading the status of women in India. Women in one way or the other are considered to be an institutionalized commodity. Globalization has accelerated the pace of exploration due to international trafficking in the flesh trade and electronic transactions by transactional crime syndicates.

Jospin Nirmala[4] (2003) in her paper, "Employment of Women and Its Impact on the Quality of Life of Women", who work in some how improved though there are certain hardless like less payment, more work load. Working women got more independence in decision making of the family and also improved their socioeconomic rights and enjoyed a better life style then their non-working female house wives.

Dhulasi Birundha Varadharajan[5] (2002) in her paper, "Achieving Empowerment through Women's Entrepreneurs", found that women's empowerment through attitudinal empowerment helped to improve women's status in society and strengthen their economic status. Women's entrepreneurship is to improve the welfare of women and therefore development and empowerment of women.

Rakesh.R[6] (2010) There are no two opinions in global era about the role of information technology in empowering Indian women. The application of Information technology could be viewed from three different angles. One is from expert point of view; secondly from the user point of view and last comes from the layman's point of view. Though the advocacy of the programme on National Computer literacy Mission in the Rural areas has resulted in the change of views and visions of the few Villagers yet we are far away from attaining the targets especially in the Tribal belts where the literacy level is not so high as compared to non tribal villages. We have to attain a milestone in brining the new hopes and smile among the faces of women when we think about the women empowerment.

Nirvikar Singh[7] (2004) pointed out in his study that there are two types of potential economic gains from the use of IT. First, there are both static and dynamic efficiency gains. Static gains are one – time, and come from more efficient use of scarce resources, allowing

---

[4] Jospin Nirmala (2003), "Employment of Women and Its Impact on the Quarterly, vol.21, No.3.

[5] Dhulashi Birundha Varatharajan (2000), "Achieving Empowerment through Women's Entrepreneurs". IASSI Quarterly, Vol-21. No.1.

[6] Rakesh.R (2010), "Role of Information Technology in Women Empowerment", Global Journal of Finance and Management, Vol.2, No.1, pp. 69-78.

[7] Nirvikar Singh (2004), Information Technology and Rural Development in India, University of California, Santa Cruz, USA, pp.1-7.

higher consumption in the present. It is useful to distinguish two kinds of static efficiency gains. One kind pertains to increases in operating efficiency, while the other comes from reduced transaction costs.

Ponnarasu.S[8] (2004) in his articles on "women empowerment" found that the participation of women in SHG makes a significant part of their empowerment both in social and economic aspects, most of the women are able to increase their income level and also contribute to the development of their family' many of the women are participating in the financial decisions of the family, which they were not earlier able to do.

Chattopadhyay Rachna and Ghosh Anjali[9] (2002) in their article "Predicting Entrepreneurial Success: A Socio-Psychological Study attempts to identify the psychological and socio-cultural variables which might prove to be responsible for entrepreneurial success, particularly of those entrepreneurs who could take advantage of the changed situation. The study is concluded with the findings that, achievement value along with entrepreneurial success are the most efficient predictor variables in predicting entrepreneurial success.

Ganesan.R and Dilbagh Maheswari.R.C[10] (2002) in their article "Women Entrepreneurs: Problems and Prospects" identifies factors which are responsible for influencing women to become entrepreneurs; and the constraints that a woman entrepreneur or her enterprise would normally face in the course of her conducting business. The study highlights the fact that entrepreneurial trainings help women entrepreneurs to become successful. Training programs needs to be reoriented towards moulding women entrepreneurs with traits and skills to meet challenging market situations.

Manimala Mathew.J[11] (2002) in his study "Founder Characteristics and Start-up Policies of Entrepreneurial Ventures: a Comparison Between British and Indian Enterprises" examines the cross-cultural comparisons of entrepreneurial profiles to ascertain the extent of universality in entrepreneurship theory. The study also assesses theextent of influence the specific environment of a country has in the nature of its entrepreneurs and enterprises. The study concludes that cultural differences between the two countries are observed to have a great impact on the personality profile than on enterprise policies and strategies.

---

[8] Ponnarasu. S (2004), "Women empowerment" "A success in twenty first century", Kisan World, vol:31, No:12, December, pp-22.

[9] Chattopadhyay Rachna and Ghosh Anjali (2002), "Predicting Entrepreneurial Success: a Socio-Psychological Study", The Journal of Entrepreneurship Vol.11,No.1.

[10] Ganesan. R and Maheswari.R.C (2002)" Women Entrepreneurs: Problems and Prospects", The Journal of Entrepreneurship Vol:11,no:1

[11] Manimala Mathew.J (2002), "Founder Characteristics and Start-up Policies of Entrepreneurial Ventures", A Comparison Between British and Indian Enterprises, The Journal of Entrepreneurship Vol:11, no:2

PandaTapan.K[12] **(2002)** in his article "Entrepreneurial Success and Risk Perception among Small-Scale Entrepreneurs of Eastern India" explains the relationship that exists among various socio-economic variables with different success levels among the enterprises. The findings reveal that there are associations between the success levels of an enterprise with factors like technical education of the entrepreneur, occupational background of parents, previous background of the entrepreneur and capability to arrange working capital. The paper also brings out the entrepreneurs perception of risk namely, the functional risk and business risk.

Kalyani.W and Chandralekha.K[13] **(2002)** in their article "Association Between Socio-Economic Demographic Profile and involvement of Women Entrepreneurs in Their Enterprise Management" analyses the involvement of women entrepreneurs in their enterprise management; and examines the association between socio-economic and demographic characteristics and involvement of women in managing their enterprise. The paper brings forth the observation that socio-economic and demographic characteristic has a significant impact on the involvement of women entrepreneurs particularly when it comes to enterprise management. Women are found to exhibit different degrees of motivation and gave considerable time for their business. Many of them had no exposure to training and hailed from poor conditions.

Mathew.P.M.[14] **(2001)** in his article "Organizational Innovation Models for SME's; Their Suitability to Indian Situation", states that, it is organizational strength rather than technology per se is going to be the key for development of small enterprises in the developing countries. He concludes that international experience does not imply possibilities of their replication in the Indian contexts, as the Indian reality is obviously complex

1.7. Scope of the Study

This study is confined to Gobichettipalayam town in Erode District of Tamil Nadu. This study is an attempt to analysis the factor influencing the women entrepreneurs, problems faced by agricultural women entrepreneurs in agricultural sector, awareness about schemes and institutions, and the level of satisfaction in agriculture.

---

[12] Panda Tapan K. (2002), "Entrepreneurial Success and Risk Perception Among Small-Scale Entrepreneurs of Eastern India", The Journal of Entrepreneurship Vol:11, NO.2.

[13] Kalyani..W and Chandralekha. K (2002),"Association Between Socio-Economic Demographic Profile and Involvement of Women Entrepreneurs in Their Enterprise Management", The Journal of Entrepreneurship Vol:11, NO.2.

[14] Mathew. P.M (2001), "Organizational Innovation Models for SMEs: Their Suitability to Indian Situation", Asia Pacific News letter vol.XII,No.1.

1.8. Objectives of the Study

In this present study the objectives may be followed by:
1. To assess the factors influencing the women entrepreneurs to enter into agricultural sector.
2. To examine the problems faced by the women agricultural entrepreneurs.
3. To identify the various rural women agricultural entrepreneurs schemes and their level of awareness about the schemes.
4. To measure the level of satisfaction of rural women agricultural entrepreneurs.
5. To determine the finding, suggestions and conclusions of the study.

1.9. Hypothesis

On the basis of the knowledge gained during the study and review of the various relevant studies the present study aim to test the following null hypotheses.

H0.There is no significant relationship between socio economic characteristics (age, educational qualification, nature of the family, size of the family, social particulars, land ownership pattern, crop production) of the sample respondents and their awareness level in schemes of rural women entrepreneurs.

H1.There is no significant relationship between socio economic characteristics (age, educational qualification, nature of the family, size of the family, social particulars, land ownership pattern, crop production) of the sample respondents and their level of satisfaction in agricultural sector.

1.10. Methodology and Sampling Design

The present study was conducted among agricultural women entrepreneurs in Gobichettipalayam town. A sample of 150 respondents has chosen for the present study based on sampling method. The primary data have been collected through survey method by direct personal interview with 150 sample respondents.

Universe of the present study is infinite. Hence, it is decided to use convenient sampling method. Originally it was planned and collected data from 180 sample respondents. Due to incompletion and non returning of respondents, it was possible to have been 150 sample respondents as final size.

1.11. Operational Definition

The various operational definitions are given below;

1.11.1. Entrepreneurship

Entrepreneurship is equivalent to enterprise which involves the willingness to assume risks in undertaking an economic activity, particularly a new one. It may involve risk taking, decision making, although neither risk nor decision making may be of great significance.

1.11.2. Entrepreneur

The entrepreneur is a person endowed with the qualities of judgment, perseverance and knowledge of the world as well as of business; entrepreneur is treated as employer, master, merchant and undertaker but explicitly identified him with capitalist.

1.11.3. Women Entrepreneur

The government of India has defined women entrepreneurs based on women participation in equity and employment of a business enterprise. Accordingly, a women entrepreneur is defined as "an enterprise owned and controlled by a women having a minimum financial interest of 51 percent of the employment generated in the enterprise to women. Women as a owner of enterprises, could be seen in manufacturing (food products), trade (readymade garments), and service (tailoring and beauty parlors) women belong to higher, middle and low income groups with different age hailing from urban, semi-urban and rural areas, having different educational qualifications with prior experiences and with demographic profile have been the entrepreneurs in the district.

1.12. Pilot Study

The pilot study is conducted with a sample of 50 rural women entrepreneurs in agriculture during 2014-2015. In the pilot study, the interview schedule is pre-tested and refined for use in the final study. On the basis of outcome of the pilot study, appropriate modifications have been made in the final interview schedule.

1.13. Geographical Area of the Study

The geographical are of the study is confined Gobichettipalayam town.

1.14. Frame Work Analysis

In the present study it is decided to use the statistical tools like Garrett's Ranking and chi square test.

1.15. Period of the Study

This study was conducted during August 2015.

1.16. Limitations of the Study

Even though an elaborate analysis is made in the study, the study not free from limitations. The following limitations are:

1. This study is restricted only to Gobichettipalayam, so the result may not be applicable to other areas.
2. This study is based on the prevailing study of women entrepreneurs.
3. As the population of the huge. The researchers has taken only 150 samples.

1.17. Chapters Schemes

Chapter I

This chapter deals with the statement of the problem, review of the literature, scope of the study, objectives of the study, Hypotheses, Methodology, Sample design, Operation definition, Pilot study, geographical area of the study, Frame work analysis, Period of the study, Limitations of the study.

Chapter II

This chapter analysis the factors influencing the women entrepreneurs in agricultural sectors.

Chapter III

This chapter examine the various problems faced by the women entrepreneurs in agricultural sectors.

Chapter IV

This chapter analysis the level of awareness about the various schemes of rural women entrepreneurs in agriculture.

Chapter V

This chapter analysis the level of satisfaction about agricultural women entrepreneurs.

Chapter VI

This chapter reveals a summary of finding, suggestions and conclusion

CHAPTER II

FACTORS INFLUENCING THE WOMEN ENTREPRENEURS ENTER INTO THE AGRICULTURAL SECTOR

2.1. Introduction

The potential of effective contribution by women to the process of agricultural and rural development has been globally reduced by adoption of socio economic policies and programmes then tend to by less responsive to the development needs of rural women , It is now widely demonstrated that rural women, as well as men, throughout the world are engaged in an range of a productive activities essential to household welfare, agricultural productivity and economic growth. Yet women's substantial contribution continues to be systematically marginalized in conventional agricultural and economic analysis and policies, while men's contribution remain the central often the sole focus of attention.

Women are typically and wrongly still characterized as "economically inactive" in a statistical surveys of agriculture, a result that tells as more about surveys methodology than about reality. The above global characterization of the women farmers is especially true for sudan where women play significant role in crop and animal production, but their production potential is not fully utilized.

In business, the entry of women is a relatively new phenomenon, on account of the breakup of the joint family system and need for additional income to maintaining living standard on account of inflation, women began to enter the competitive world of business .A women may start her own business due to several reasons. She may not be able to find out of her house .some women may not start their own business as they are stagnating near the top male owned firms.

In recent years women have their marks in different walks of life and are competing successfully with men despite the social, psychological and economic barriers. This has been possible due to education, political awakening, urbanization, legal safeguards, social reforms etc. Some of the women have distinguished themselves in many unconventional fields as prime minister, Ambassadors, Governors, Space scientists, Pilots, Vice chancellors, Administrators and Entrepreneurs.

Women entrepreneurs are observed dealing with production of both consumer goods and intermediate goods or articles like a male entrepreneurs a women entrepreneurs also requires to perform the functions of exploring the prospects of starting new enterprise undertaking of risks and handling of economic uncertainities, introduction of innovation, co-ordination, control and change management.

While collect the data in the interview schedule the factors like:

- Additional income for the family
- High profit factor
- To continue the family business
- To available the government loan
- To self secure employment/independent living
- Own interest
- Social status/prestige in society
- To improved standard of living
- Easy to start
- Unique idea/No competition
- Technological knowledge/training of present business line
- Nearness to market

Additional Income for the Family

Income is very essential for each and every human being and also to run the family smoothly. Hence the income is very one of the important factor for women to become on entrepreneurs. In modern days the family expenses going on increasing, to meet the excess expense to women become an entrepreneurs.

High Profit Factor

The aim of the business to earn profit. It includes the women to start a business to earn a profit. It also one of the important factors for women to become an entrepreneurs.

To Continue the Family Business

The women entrepreneurs are to continue or maintain their family business. They wished to continue their family business due to death of their family members.

To Available the Government Loan

It is most important factor for women to become an entrepreneur, the government is ready to provide a loan to the women entrepreneur, so the women entrepreneurs use the facility given by government to start a business.

To Secure Self Employment

Now a days everyone has need a job to survive in the society, because the economic level is increased day by day. Women entrepreneurs have some courage and confidents to face any problems in their business.

Own Interest

Out of her interest every women has to start their business. This is one of the important factors for women to become an entrepreneur.

Social Status/Prestige in Society

Women entrepreneur are ready to start a business for maintaining the prestige in society. At the same time women's are exposed their talents to the society.

To Improved Standard of Living

Women start business to develop their standard of living . It is one of the important factor for women entrepreneur.

Easy to Start

Women have more facility to become an entrepreneur then man, women have more opportunity in every place. Women easily claims loan from the bank then men, so the women can start the business easily.

Unique Idea/No Competition

In the modern world all business has competition, but for a particular business which is carried out by women has less competition.

Technical Knowledge

Everyone have some special kind of technical knowledge, skills, ability and they have some special training for doing a particular business.

Nearness to Market

Marketing of a product is facing some problem without taking more risk to sale the products, they can sale the products easily, because the market is nearest to the business unit.

Against the background, in the present study it is decided analysis the factors influencing the women entrepreneurs to choose their careers. To identify the most significant factor, respondents were asked to rank their choice.

On the basis of such ranking for analysis purpose, Garrett Ranking techniques was used for which the following formula

Garret's Ranking formula:[15]   Present Position $= \dfrac{100(R_{ij} - 0.5)}{N_j}$

Where

Rij = Rank given for the ith factor by the sample respondents,

Nj = Number of factor Ranked by j[th] respondents.

Table 2.1: Factors Influencing of Women Agriculture Entrepreneurs: Garrett's Ranking Techniques

Factors	Rank	1	2	3	4	5	6	7	8	9	10	11	12	Total Score	Mean Score	Rank
	Score Valve	96	72	66	60	56	52	47	43	39	34	27	16			
1.Additional income for the family	F	48	36	84	48	36	48	36	48	36	60	36	48	600	51.91	VI
	FX	4608	2592	5544	2880	2016	4368	1692	2256	1404	2040	972	768	31140		
2.High profit factor	F	36	72	48	36	60	84	36	36	48	68	28	48	600	51.32	V
	FX	3456	5184	3168	2160	3360	4368	1692	1548	1872	2312	7236	768	30788		
3.Own Interest	F	56	28	36	24	92	60	72	68	36	76	28	24	150	51.98	IV
	FX	5376	2016	2376	1440	5152	3120	3384	3196	1404	2584	756	384	31188		
4.Self employment	F	84	60	24	48	32	24	44	80	84	36	48	36	600	53.48	II
	FX	8064	4320	1584	2880	1792	1248	2068	3760	3276	2412	1296	576	32088		
5.To available the government loan	F	32	48	60	24	72	28	96	52	48	28	72	40	600	49.12	IX
	FX	3072	3456	3960	1440	4032	1456	4512	2444	1872	952	1944	640	29708		
6.To continue the family business	F	84	68	24	52	44	72	32	24	112	36	28	20	600	55.64	I
	FX	8064	4896	1584	3120	2464	3952	1504	1128	4368	1224	756	320	33380		
7.Prestige in society	F	36	40	72	116	40	20	28	72	28	28	36	84	600	50.17	VII
	FX	3456	2880	4752	6960	2240	1040	1312	3096	1092	952	972	1344	30100		
8.To improved standard of living	F	48	36	92	72	64	32	52	36	44	64	28	32	600	53.32	III
	FX	4608	2592	6072	4320	3584	1664	2444	1548	1716	2176	756	512	31992		
9.Easy to start	F	24	80	36	24	36	28	72	48	56	48	100	48	600	46.81	X
	FX	2304	5760	2376	1440	2016	1456	3384	2064	2184	1632	2700	768	28084		
10.Unique idea	F	68	56	44	28	20	32	56	56	52	88	44	56	600	50.12	VIII
	FX	6528	4032	2904	1680	1120	1664	1120	2632	2408	2992	2992	1188	30076		
11.Technical knowledge	F	36	32	32	60	24	68	48	48	80	44	64	64	600	44.71	XI
	FX	3240	2304	2112	3600	1248	3196	2064	1872	2720	1496	1728	1024	27000		
12.Nearness to market	F	48	44	48	68	80	64	28	32	28	24	36	100	600	43.31	XII
	FX	4608	3168	3168	4080	4160	3008	1204	1248	952	816	972	1600	28984		
TOTAL		600	600	600	600	600	600	600	600	600	600	600	600			

x=score value, f=sample of respondents, fx= mean score

By referring the Garrett's table the percent position estimated to converted into scores. Then for each factors, the scores of each individual are added and then mean value calculated. The factors having highest mean value is considered to the most important.

---

[15] Selvaraj.A (2005), "Cultivation and marketing problems of jasmine in Erode district of Tamil Nadu", un published Ph.D., dissertation submitted to Bharathiar university, Coimbatore.

It is observed from the table 2.1 that the to continue the family business with high mean score of 55.64 is proved to be the most important factor to motivate the factors influencing women entrepreneurs, self employment is mean score of 53.48 ranked as second, improved standard of living mean score of 53.32 ranked as third. And other factors followed by own interest, high profit factor, prestige in society, nearness to market, easy to start, prestige in society, to available the government loan, unique idea, technological knowledge.

CHAPTER III

PROBLEMS FACED BY RURAL WOMEN ENTREPRENEURS IN AGRICULTURAL SECTOR

3.1. Introduction

Women entrepreneurs face a series of problems right from the beginning till the enterprise functions. Being a woman itself poses various problems to a woman entrepreneur. The problems of Indian women pertains to her responsibility towards family, society and lion work.

The tradition, customs, socio cultural values, ethics, motherhood subordinates to ling husband and men, physically weak, hard work areas, feeling of insecurity, cannot be tough etc are some peculiar problems that the Indian women are coming across while they jump into entrepreneurship.

Women in rural areas have to suffer still further. They face tough resistance from men. They are considered as helpers. The attitude of society towards her and constraints in which she has to live and work are not very conducive. While collect the data in the interview schedule problems of women agricultural entrepreneurs like:

- Lack of self confident
- Irrigation/monsoon
- Discouragement of family members and others
- Problem of finance
- Male domination
- Lack of education
- Health problem
- Problem in marketing
- Lack of awareness of government policies
- No direct ownership of the property

Lack of Self Confidence

Women entrepreneurs because of their inherent nature, lack of self-confidence which is essentially a motivating factor in running an enterprise successfully. They have to strive hard to strike a balance between managing a family and managing an enterprise. Sometimes she has to sacrifice her entrepreneurial urge in order to strike a balance between the two.

Women entrepreneurs are not confident about their strength and competence. Their family members don't stand by their entrepreneurial growth. In recent years, though the situation is changing, yet the women have to face further change for increased entrepreneurial growth

Irrigation or Monsoon

We are all know that Indian agriculture is dependent on monsoon, which is uncertain, unreliable and erratic. This problem provide the need for proper irrigation system, if monsoon are good , the entire economy is upbeat and when the monsoon fails, every one, every where takes a hit to some extent.

Discouragement from Family Members/Others

In India, it is mainly a women's duty to look after the children and other members of the family. Man plays a secondary role only. In case of married women, she has to strike a fine balance between her business and family. Her total involvement in family leaves little or no energy and time to devote for business.

Women in India are very emotionally attached to their families. They are supposed to attend to all the domestic work, to look after the children and other members of the family. They are over burden with family responsibilities like extra attention to husband, children and in laws which take away a lots of their time and energy. In such situation, it will be very difficult to concentrate and run the enterprise successfully

Problem of Finance

Finance is regarded as "life blood" for any enterprise, be it big or small. However, women entrepreneurs suffer from shortage of finance on two counts. Firstly, women do not generally have property on their names to use them as collateral for obtaining funds from external sources. Thus, their access to the external sources of funds is limited. Secondly, the banks also consider women less credit- worthy and discourage women borrowers on the belief that they can at any time leave their business. Given such situation, women entrepreneurs are bound to rely on their own savings, if any and loans from friends.

Male Domination

Even though our constitution speaks of equality between sexes, male chauvinism is still the order of the day. Women are not treated equal to men. Their entry to business requires the approval of the head of the family. Entrepreneurship has traditionally been seen as a male preserve. All these puts a break in the growth of women entrepreneurs

Lack of Education

Women in India are lagging far behind in the field of education. Most of the women (around sixty per cent of total women) are illiterate. Those who are educated are provided either less or inadequate education than their male counterpart partly due to early marriage, partly due to son's higher education and partly due to poverty. Due to lack of proper education, women entrepreneurs remain in dark about the development of new technology, new methods of production, marketing and other governmental support which will encourage them to flourish.

Health Problems

Major health problems faced by women entrepreneurs were tension, backache, eyestrain fatigue and headache. It is found that women feeling the problem of feeling fatigued after returning home, lack of rest and sleep and heavy schedule.

Marketing Problems

Women entrepreneurs continuously face the problems in marketing their products. For marketing the products women entrepreneurs have to be at the mercy of middlemen who pocket the chunk of profit. Although the middlemen exploit the women entrepreneurs, the elimination of middlemen is difficult, because it involves a lot of running about. Women entrepreneurs also find it difficult to capture the market and make their products popular.

Lack of Awareness of Government policies

Government gives great support for entrepreneurial development especially in rural areas. It also runs special programmes and schemes for women. The support from government comes by way of financial, technical support, and assistance in procuring raw material, establishment of entrepreneurial unit and in other ways like subsidies, concessions and tax rebates. Cent percent respondents of both the category, as shown in table 4 did not have any idea about any of such schemes accept that the banks and financial institutes provide loans. 36.67 percent entrepreneurial women and 80 percent non-entrepreneurial women reported that they do not get information timely

No Direct Ownership of the Property

No doubt, the right of property is given as a legal provision in India, but it raises one of the most important questions regarding the right to property for women. There are very few women having on paper the right of property because, firstly, they are not aware of this right. They only become aware when problems are created in their families due to family disputes.

Otherwise, women are not enjoying their right of property, being treated as second-class citizens, which keeps them in a "pervasive cycle of poverty".

Against the background, in the present study it is decided analysis the problems faced by the women entrepreneurs in agricultural sector. To identify the most significant factor, respondents were asked to rank their choice.

On the basis of such ranking for analysis purpose, Garrett Ranking techniques was used for which the following formula;

Garret's Ranking Formula : Present position $= \dfrac{100(R_{ij} - 0.5)}{N_j}$

Where

R_{ij} = Rank given for the ith factor by the sample respondents,

N_j = Number of factor Ranked by j^{th} respondents.

Table 3.1: Problems Faced by Women Agriculture Entrepreneurs: Garrett's Ranking Techniques

Problems	Rank / Score Valve	1 / 81	2 / 70	3 / 63	4 / 57	5 / 52	6 / 47	7 / 42	8 / 36	9 / 29	10 / 18	Total Score	Mean Score	Rank
Lack of self confidence	F	24	48	72	96	108	48	48	36	84	36	600	46.31	X
	FX	1944	3360	4536	5472	5616	2256	2016	1296	2436	648	29580		
Irrigation/monsoon	F	36	72	48	48	96	108	36	24	48	84	600	46.82	IX
	FX	2961	5040	3024	2736	4992	5076	1512	864	1392	1512	29109		
Problem of finance	F	84	48	96	96	48	36	48	48	56	40	600	53.27	I
	FX	6804	3360	6048	5472	2496	1692	2016	1728	1624	720	31900		
No direct ownership of the property	F	36	112	28	24	52	76	60	64	72	60	600	47.63	VI
	FX	2916	7840	1764	1368	2704	3572	2520	2304	2088	1080	28156		
Lack of self confidence	F	48	52	64	48	28	92	64	72	72	60	600	47.54	VII
	FX	3888	3640	4032	2736	1456	4324	2688	2592	2088	1080	28524		
Lack of awareness of government olicies	F	48	48	112	44	36	64	84	120	24	20	600	50.99	IV
	FX	3888	3360	7056	2508	1872	3008	3528	4320	696	360	30596		
Lack of education	F	108	36	64	60	44	32	80	52	44	76	600	50.65	III
	FX	8748	2520	4032	3420	2288	1504	3360	1872	1276	1368	7597		
Discourage from family members	F	96	24	52	52	40	48	64	56	56	112	600	47.3	VIII
	FX	7776	1680	3276	2964	2080	2256	2688	2016	1624	2016	30388		
Problems in marketing	F	72	84	32	68	68	24	72	56	48	76	600	50.12	II
	FX	5832	5880	2016	3876	3536	1128	3024	2016	1372	1368	30068		
Health problem	F	48	76	32	64	80	72	44	72	80	32	600	49.6	V
	FX	3888	5320	2016	3846	4160	3384	1848	2592	2320	576	29752		
TOTAL		600	600	600	600	600	600	600	600	600	600			

x=score value, f=sample of respondents, fx= mean score

It is observed from the table 3.1 that the major problem felt by the sample respondents are problem of finance as indicated by its highest mean score value 53.27 this is followed by problem in marketing mean score of 50.12 is ranked as second, lack of education mean score value 50.65 is ranked as third. And other problems are followed by lack of awareness of government policies, no direct ownership of the property, health problems, irrigation/ monsoon, lack of self confidents, male domination, discouragement from family members.

CHAPTER IV

VARIOUS SCHEMES AND INSTITUTIONS OF WOMEN ENTREPRENEURS IN AGRICULTURAL SECTOR AND THEIR AWARENESS LEVEL

4.1. Introduction

The Government can influence both economic and non-economic field for the entrepreneurs through its actions. Any interested Government can help in economic development through different policies. Government can provide a facilitative socio economic setting for women entrepreneurs. Such conductive settings minimize the risk entrepreneurs are to encounter. Compassionate actions of the Government can therefore be considered as the most advantageous for entrepreneurial growth. Similarly, negative governmental actions, such as colonial disruption, act as inhibiting factors of entrepreneurial development. Commitment of the Government can flourish entrepreneurship development in any country. However, women entrepreneurship was for a long time not considered to be important for economic development. Despite progress, there is still need and scope for the Government of Bangladesh to takes some rural entrepreneurship development policies and rules that would flourish women entrepreneurship.

The all round development of women has been one of the focal point of planning process in India.

The **First Five-Year Plan (1951-56)** envisaged a number of welfare measures for women. Establishment of the Central Social Welfare Board, organization of Mahila Mandals and the Community Development Programmes were a few steps in this direction.

In the **Second Five-Year Plan (1956-61)**, the empowerment of women was closely linked with the overall approach of intensive agricultural development programmes.

The **Third and Fourth Five-Year Plans (1961-66 and 1969-74)** supported female education as a major welfare measure.

The **Fifth Five-Year Plan (1974-79)** emphasized training of women, who were in need of income and protection. This plan coincided with International Women's Decade and the submission of Report of the Committee on the Status of Women in India. In 1976, Women's welfare and Development Bureau was set up under the Ministry of Social Welfare.

The **Sixth Five-Year Plan (1980-85)** saw a definite shift from welfare to development. It recognized women's lack of access to resources as a critical factor impending their growth.

The **Seventh Five-Year Plan (1985-90)** emphasized the need for gender equality and empowerment. For the first time, emphasis was placed upon qualitative aspects such as inculcation of confidence, generation of awareness with regards, to rights and training in skills for better employment.

The **Eight Five-Year Plan (1992-97)** focused on empowering women, especially at the grass roots level, through Panchayath Raj Institutions.

The **Ninth Five-Year Plan (1997-2002)** adopted a strategy of women's component plan, under which not less than 30 percent of funds/benefits were earmarked for women-specific programmes.

The Plan **Tenth Five-Year plan (2002-07)** aims at empowering women through translating the recently adopted National Policy for Empowerment of Women (2001) into action and ensuring Survival, Protection and Development of women and children through rights based approach.

The **Eleventh Five-Year** Plan lays down six monitor able targets (1) Raise the sex ratio for age group 0–6 from 927 in 2001 to 935 by 2011–12 and to 950 by 2016–17; (2) Ensure that at least 33% of the direct and indirect beneficiaries of all government schemes are women and girl children; (3) Reduce IMR from 57 to 28 and MMR from 3.01 to one per 1000 live births; (4) Reduce malnutrition among children of age group 0–3 to half its present level; (5) Reduce malnutrition among women and girls by 50% by the end of the Eleventh Plan; and (6) Reduce dropout rate for primary and secondary schooling by 10% for both girls as well as boys.

4.2.   Schemes of Rural Women Entrepreneurship

For empowerment of women and all round development of women the Ministries of Government of India has come up with various schemes time to time. These schemes are either central, state specific or joint collaboration between the centre and states. Some of the schemes are followed by:

1.   Rural Entrepreneurship Development Programmes (REDP)
2.   Integrated Rural Development Programme(IRDP)
3.   Development of Women And Children in Rural Areas(DWCRA)
4.   Training of Rural Youth for Self Employment(TRYSEM)
5.   Support of Training and Employment Programme(STEP)
6.   Mahila Samriddhi Yojana(MSY)
7.   Women's Development Corporation(WDC)

8. The National Policy For Empowerment of Women

9. Norwegian Agency for Development(NORAD)

10. The National Bank for Agricultural and Rural Development(NABARD)

11. Swarnajayanthi Gram Swarozgar(SGSY)

12. Rajiv Gandhi National Creche Scheme

13. TREAD Subcidy Schemes For Women

14. Prime Ministers Rozgar Yojana(PMRY)

15. Indhira Mahila Yojana(IMY)

16. Rashtirya Mahila Kosh(RMK)

17. Krishi Vigyan Kendra(KVK)

18. Tamil Nadu Corporation for Development of Women

4.2.1. Rural Entrepreneurship Development Programmes (REDPs)

Under this programme, grant assistance is sanctioned to reputed Voluntary Agencies (Vas) and professional agencies for conducting REDPs. It envisages the agency to provide 2 years escort and follow-up support to the trained women. In addition to REDPs, master-craftswomen also sanction special training programmes covering skill up gradation, market-oriented training programmes and training of and by master-craftswomen.

The Rural Entrepreneurship Development Programmes (REDPs) in India have been institutionalized by the Entrepreneurship Development Institute of India, Ahmedabad. The civil society institutions, particularly the Non Governmental Organisations (NGOs), are seen as agents who help state agenciesin implementing the programmes. The motivation, training and the follow up component is the role state expects NGOs to undertake3. EDP's are designed to support a person or group wishing to start a business. It inculcates in the entrepreneur the necessary entrepreneurial traits that develop the personnel, financial, technical, managerial and marketing capabilities and skills. The main objective of integrated rural development programmes is to increase the income generating power of the family who are below the poverty line to alleviate the poverty 30 percent women should be the beneficiaries in rural development programmes run by the government.

4.2.2. Integrated Rural Development Programme (IRDP)

The Integrated Rural Development Programme (IRDP) was launched on 20th October 1980, as a major credit linked self employment programme for poverty alleviation. The objective of the programme is to identify rural poor families, to augment their income and to enable them to cross the poverty line through acquisition of employment on a sustainable basis. Assistance is given in the form of subsidy by the Government and credit advances by financial institutions for income generating activities in the rural areas.

4.2.3. Development of Women and Children in Rural Areas (DWCRA)

DWCRA, a sub-component of IRDP was launched as a pilot project in 1982-83 in selected districts throughout the country. The objective of the program is to organize women in socio-economic activity groups with the dual objective of strengthening them.

Groups of 15 to 20 women are formed and a grant of Rs.15,000 given to them as a revolving fund for purchase of raw materials, marketing, childcare, etc. Multipurpose community centres are constructed for the women to carry out their economic activities. DWCRA also aims to increase these women's access to other government programs and welfare services.

4.2.4. Training of Rural Youth for Self Employment (TRYSEM)

TRYSEM is a supporting component of the IRDP. The main objective of this scheme is to equip rural youth with the necessary technical and entrepreneurial skills through a training institution or a master craftsman, so as to enable them to take up income generating activities. Out of the total number of beneficiaries under the scheme, at least 40 per cent should be women. To enable the participants to take up employment, a suitable tool kit costing more than Rs800 is also provided. The scheme aimed at training about two lakhs rural youth in the country every year in various skills. Training of rural women is also given due consideration.

4.2.5. Support of Training and Employment Programme (STEP)

This programme seeks to provide skills and new knowledge to poor and assetless women in the traditional sectors. Under this project, women beneficiaries are organized into viable and cohesive groups or cooperatives. A comprehensive package of services such as health care, elementary education, crèche facility, market linkages, etc. are provided besides access to credit. Skill development is provided in ten traditional skills amongst women. This is a Central Scheme launched in 1987. The Ministry is at present getting the programme evaluated. Based on the results of the evaluation, the scheme is proposed to be revamped.

4.2.6. Mahila Samriddhi Yojana (MSY)

MSY was launched on 2nd Oct 1993, to promote self reliance and a measure of economic independence among rural women by encouraging thrift. Under the scheme, every adult rural woman is encouraged to have an account in the post office under the jurisdiction of her village. The scheme has received a very enthusiastic response from both rural and tribal women including from those living in the remote areas of the country as reported by Department of Women and Child Welfare, New Delhi.

4.2.7. Women's Development Corporations (WDCs)

This scheme was sanctioned by the Government of India in 1986-87 for setting the pace for self employment among women and to main stream them into the development process. The aim of these corporations is to provide technical, managerial, marketing and financial information for the weaker sections of women so that they can generate a sustained income for themselves. The main functions of the corporations are to facilitate the availability of credit through banks and other financial institutions.

4.2.8. The National Policy for Empowerment of Women

The Government of India has declared 2001 as Women's Empowerment year. The national policy of empowerment of women has set certain clear-cut goals and objectives. The policy aims at upliftment, development and empowerment in socio-economic and politico–cultural aspects, by creating in them awareness on various issues in relation to their empowerment.

4.2.9. Norwegian Agency for Development

NORAD for training and skill development, and also for promotion of self-reliance through the generation of income for women in nontraditional trades. Since 1982-83 when the programme was launched, till 31 December 1997, 1.40 lakh women have been benefited through 887 projects.

4.2.10. The National Bank for Agricultural and Rural Development

(NABARD), with the objective of meeting the credit needs of the poor links banks with self help groups. About 85 per cent of the self help groups that linked with the banks are women's groups. The Scheme for setting up Women's Development Corporations in States was formulated, in 1986-87 with a view to identifying women entrepreneurs, providing them with technical consultancy, facilitating availability of credits, promoting marketing of products, strengthening women's cooperatives, arranging training facilities, etc. The scheme was transferred to the State sector during 1992-93, as per the decision of the National Development Council.

4.2.11. Swarnajayanthi Gram Swarozgar (SGSY)

The Swarnajayanti Gram Swarozgar Yojana (SGSY) was launched in April 1999 after restructuring the Integrated Rural Development Programme (IRDP) and allied programmes. It is the only Self Employment Programme currently being implemented for the rural poor. The objective of the SGSY is to bring the assisted swarozgar is above the poverty line by providing them income generating assets through bank credit and government subsidy. The scheme is being implemented on cost sharing basis of 75:25 between the Centre and States.

4.2.12. Rajiv Gandhi National Creche Scheme

Rajiv Gandhi National Creche Scheme-With a view to encourage women to join/continue with gainful employment, Rajiv Gandhi National Creche Scheme for children of working mothers (RGNCS) was introduced in 2006. The scheme seeks to provide day care facilities to children in the age group 0-6 years from families with a monthly income of less than Rs. 12,000/-. In addition to being a safe space for the children, the crèche provide services like supplementary nutrition, pre school education, emergency health care etc.

The scheme provides for grant of Rs.3532/- per month for a crèche, limited to 90% of the schematic pattern or actual expenditure whichever is less, and the remaining expenditure is borne by the implementing agencies. Honorarium to crèche workers is fully funded under the scheme. Funds are separately provided to the implementing agencies for one time training of crèche workers.

4.2.13. Tread Subsidy scheme for Women

Trade Related Entrepreneurship Assistance and Development (TREAD) Scheme for Women is a subsidy in India provided by the Ministry of Micro, Small & Medium Enterprises. Government provides subsidy of up to 30% of the total project cost as appraised by lending institutions which would finance the remaining 70% as loan Assistance to applicant women. Women eligible under this scheme are who have no easy access to credit from banks due to their cumbersome procedures and the inability of poor & usually illiterate/semi-literate women to provide adequate security demanded by banks in the form of collaterals. Further, the request for subsidy under this scheme must be made by a NGO for a number of individual or group(s) women.

4.2.14. Indira Mahila Yojana (IMY)

The scheme has received a very enthusiastic response from both rural and tribal women including from those living in the remote areas of the country as reported by Department of Women and Child Welfare, New Delhi. Women development programme initiated by the Government, which was launched in August 1995 in more than 200 blocks of the country. It was launched in 1995.

4.2.15. Indira Mahila Yojana (IMY)

The scheme has received a very enthusiastic response from both rural and tribal women including from those living in the remote areas of the country as reported by Department of Women and Child Welfare, New Delhi. Women development programme initiated by the Government, which was launched in August 1995 in more than 200 blocks of the country. It was launched in 1995.

4.2.16. Rashtriya Mahila Kosh (RMK)

RMK was set up as a registered society in March 1993. It is intended to meet the credit needs of poor women particularly in the informal sector. It is being managed by a governing board which has approved the policies and procedures for lending to women borrowers through the intermediation of NGOs and other women's organizations like co-operative societies, women development corporations, etc., for which suitable eligibility criteria such as lending and credit management experience and sound financial management have been prescribed.

4.2.17. Krishi Vigyan Kendra

ICAR sponsored KVK are available throughout the country, conducting various vocational training programme with broad objective of promoting agripreneurship among farm youth. Eg. Some of the novel Training programme like Production of organic products and organic inputs, Special packaged foods for Sugar patient, Heart patient, packaged flower for special occasion and season promotes business entrepreneurship. It was launched in 2004.

Apart from this the KVK has also prepared visual material accessible for the farmers that comprises 14-multimedia presentation and one audio presentation called Tomato Extension and Training Information System. The information that is required by the farmers has been compiled specifically in Marathi for the farmers to facilitate easy understanding of the improved crop cultivation practices related to various crops grown by them. In all 646 women farmers from 4 villages availed the facilities of IT Centres for information which include 246 for technology, 98 for market information, 33 for weather and 269 for other information.

4.2.18. Tamil Nadu Corporation for Development of Women

Tamil Nadu Corporation for development of women was established in 1983 which aims at the socio-economic empowerment of women. As a prelude, the Corporation is implementing the Mahalir Thittam among poor rural women to promote saving habits, nurture entrepreneurial skills and aptitudes, promote exposure to banking transactions and to free them from the clutches of local moneylenders. The scheme is being implemented in partnership with Non-Governmental Organisations (NGOs) and Banks. Under the scheme, SHGs are formed and monitored through NGOs affiliated with the Tamil Nadu Corporations for Development of Women, Ltd.

4.3. Qualifications of Data to Measure the Awareness Level of Women Entrepreneurs in Agricultural Sectors

A comprehensive interview schedule is design to collect the data from the sample respondents. Likert's type 2 point rating scale is applied. To measure the awareness level about awareness, a list of 18 statements was given in interview schedule are prepared.

As per likert type 2 point rating scale ranges from 2 and 1 are used. If a represents is more awareness about a statement, a scale value of 2 is assigned. Scale value 1 is assigned to if respondents are unaware.

A total score for each respondents from all 18 statements are calculated by using the likert's 2 point rating scale technique. The maximum score of a respondents will be from al the 15 statements.

The respondents are grouped on the basis of score into 2 viz, aware and unaware. Those who have scored below 21 are classified as low and their opinion about women entrepreneur's awareness level is low. Those who have scored between 21 and 60 (i.e) their opinion of women entrepreneur's level is high.

4.4. Measuring the Institutional and Schemes Awareness of Women Entrepreneurs in Agricultural Sectors

In this present study, awareness about women entrepreneurs has been analyzed by giving 18 statements findings have been convert into score as per qualification procedure as stated in findings relating to institutions and schemes awareness are shown in a table

Table 4.1: Distribution of Sample Respondents According to Awareness Level

Awareness level	No. of the Respondents	Percentage
Unaware	440	73.3
Aware	160	26.7
Total	600	100

Table 4.1 shows that the level of awareness are 440 sample respondents are unaware about the schemes, and 160 sample respondents are aware about the schemes in agricultural sector.

Association between Socio-Economic Characteristics of the Sample Respondents and Level of Awareness about Institutions and Schemes

It is expected that socio-economic characteristics of the sample respondents would influence the level of awareness about women entrepreneurs in agricultural sector. The following hypothesis has been framed on the basis of the review of the relevant studies and the outcome of the pilot study.

H0: There is no significant relationship between socio economic characteristics (age, educational qualification, size of family, type of family, social particulars, land ownership pattern, crop production) of the sample respondents and awareness level of the sample respondents.

4.4.1. Age and Awareness Level

Age is an important factor which may influence the agriculture women's. The present study is an attempt to relationship between age and awareness level. It is found that the sample respondents age ranges from 18 years to 50 years. In the present study, sample respondents are grouped into young, middle and old categories.

Table 4.2: Distribution of Sample Respondents according to Age and Awareness Level

Age group	Awareness level		Total
	High	Low	
Young	100(90.91)	20(9.09)	120(100)
Middle	160(70.89)	120(29.41)	280(100)
Old	180(65)	20(35)	200(100)
Total	440	160	600

Figure in paranthesis indicates percentage, D.f 2 χ^2=4.6

As per the table 4.2 it is clear that in a sample of 600 respondents, 100 sample respondents were belonging from the category of young age group, 160 sample respondents were belonging from middle age group and 180 sample respondents were belonging from old age group having low level of awareness.

To test the significance between age of the respondents and awareness level of the χ^2 test was applied. The calculated value (4.6) of chi-square is less than table value (5.9). Hence the hypothesis is accepted. It can be concluded that there is no significant association between the age and awareness level of the sample respondents about women agricultures and schemes.

4.4.2. Educational Qualification and Awareness Level

Educational qualification is an important factor which may influence the agricultural women entrepreneurs. Education is a vital factor for the socio economic development. An education not only widens knowledge but also helps a person to make use of rational and scientific approach to solve problems.

Therefore, it is expected that there may be a relationship between Educational level of the women agricultures and their level of awareness about the schemes. The present study is an attempt to relationship between educational qualification and awareness level. In the present study, a sample respondents are grouped into illiterate, school level, college level, professionals categories.

Table 4.3: Distribution of Sample Respondents according to Educational Qualification and Awareness Level

Educational Qualification	Awareness level		Total
	High	Low	
Illiterate	200(90.2)	20(9.08)	220(100)
School level	100(68.35)	72(31.65)	172(100)
College level	100(78.14)	40(21.86)	140(100)
Professionals	40(43.26)	28(56.74)	68(100)
Total	440	160	6000

Figure in paranthesis indicates percentage, D.F 2 χ^2 =5.8

As per the table 4.3 it is clear that in a sample 600 respondents 200 sample respondents were belonging from illiterate,100 sample respondents were belonging from school level, 100 sample respondents were belonging from college level and 40 sample respondents were belonging from professionals having low level of awareness.

To test the significance between educational qualification of the and awareness level of the χ^2 test was applied. The calculation value (5.8) of chi-square is less than table value (6.1) Hence, the hypothesis is accepted. It can be concluded that there is no significant association between the education qualification and awareness level of the sample respondents about women agricultures and schemes.

4.4.3. Nature of Family and Awareness Level

Type of family is an important factor which may influence the agriculture women entrepreneurs. The present study is an attempt to relationship between type of family and awareness level. It is found that the sample respondents families are converted into joint family and nuclear family.

Table 4.4: Distribution of Sample Respondents according to Nature of Family and Awareness
Level

Nature of family	Awareness level		Total
	High	**low**	
Joint	256(74.35)	72(25.65)	328 (100)
Nuclear	184(58.65)	88(41.35)	272(100)
Total	440	160	600

Figure in paranthesis indicates percentage, D.F 2 χ^2 =4.7

As per the table 4.4 it is clear that in a sample of 600 respondents,256 sample respondents
were belonging from joint family184 sample respondents were belonging from Nuclear family
having low level of awareness.

To test the significance between age of the respondents and awareness level of the χ^2 test
was applied. The calculation value (4.7) of chi-square is greater than table value (3.8). Hence,
the hypothesis is not accepted. It can be concluded that there is no significant association
between the nature of family and awareness level of the sample respondents about women
agricultures and schemes.

4.4.4. *Size of Family and Awareness Level*

Size of family is an important factor which may influence the agriculture women
entrepreneurs. A family is defined as a group of persons, all related to each other. The number
of members in it constitutes a family's size. If there is more number of members in the family, it
is possible to do some activities which concerns about the agriculture. The size of the family
reflects on the economic status of the farmers and this plays an important role in determining
the viability of agriculture.

Number of members in the farmers family ranged from 2 to 8.The present study is an
attempt to relationship between size of family and awareness level. It is found that the sample
respondents family sizes from the sample respondents are grouped into small, medium and
large categories.

Table 4.5: Distribution of Sample Respondents according to Size of the Family and Awareness
Level

Size of family	Awareness level		Total
	High	**Low**	
Small	120 (74.6)	52(25.4)	172(100)
Medium	192 (62.25)	76(37.75)	268(100)
Large	128(81.15)	32(18.85)	160(100)
Total	440	160	600

Figure in paranthesis indicates percentage, D.F 2 χ^2 =5.4

As per the table 4.5 it is clear that in a sample of 600 respondents 120 sample respondents were belonging small, 192 sample respondents were belonging from medium and 128 sample respondents were belonging from large families having low level of awareness.

To test the significance between age of the respondents and awareness level of the χ^2 test was applied. The calculation value (5.4) of chi-square is greater than table value (4.01) Hence, the hypothesis is not accepted. It can be concluded that there is no significant association between the size of family and awareness level of the sample respondents about women agricultures and schemes.

4.4.5. *Social Particulars*

Social particulars is an important factor which may influence the agriculture women's. The present study is an attempt to relationship between social particulars and awareness level. It is found that the sample respondents are divided into no participants, participants and public leaders.

Table 4.6: Distribution of Sample Respondents according to Social Particulars and Awareness Level

Social particulars	Awareness level		Total
	High	Low	
No participants	200 (74.6)	80(25.4)	280(100)
participants	120(62.25)	48(37.75)	168(100)
Public leader	160(81.15)	32(18.85)	192(100)
Total	440	160	600

Figure in paranthesis indicates percentage, D.F 2 χ^2 =6.3

As per the table 4.6 it is clear that in a sample of 600 respondents, 200 sample respondents were belonging from the category of No participants, 120 sample respondents were belonging from participated and 160 sample respondents were belonging from public leaders having low level of awareness.

To test the significance between age of the respondents and awareness level of the χ^2 test was applied. The calculation value (6.3) of chi-square is less than table value(7.1) Hence, the hypothesis is accepted. It can be concluded that there is no significant association between the social particulars and awareness level of the sample respondents about women agricultures and schemes.

4.4.6. Land Ownership Pattern and Awareness Level

Land ownership pattern is an important factor which may influence the agriculture women entrepreneurs. The present study is an attempt to relationship between land ownership pattern and awareness level. In the present study, a sample respondents are grouped into No land, own land, Leased in and Leased out, middle and old categories.

Table 4.7: Distribution of Sample Respondents according to Land Ownership and Awareness Level

Land ownership pattern	Awareness level		Total
	High	Low	
No land	200(90.2)	20(9.08)	220(100)
Own land	100(68.35)	72 (31.65)	172(100)
Leased in	100(78.14)	40(21.86)	140(100)
Leased out	40(43.26)	28(56.74)	68(100)
Total	440	160	600

Figure in paranthesis indicates percentage, D.F 2 χ^2 =4.6

As per the table 4.7 it is clear that in a sample of 600 respondents, 200 sample respondents were belonging from the category of No land, 100 sample respondents were belonging from Own land, 100 sample respondents were belonging from Leased in and 40 percent were belonging from Leased out having low level of awareness.

To test the significance between age of the respondents and awareness level of the χ^2 test was applied. The calculation value (4.6) of chi-square is less than table value (5.1). Hence, the hypothesis is accepted. It can be concluded that there is no significant association between the land ownership and awareness level of the sample respondents about women agricultures and schemes.

4.4.7. Crop Production and Awareness Level

Crop production is an important factor which may influence the agriculture women entrepreneurs. The present study is an attempt to relationship between crop production and awareness level. In the present study, a sample respondents are grouped into No crop production, Small, Medium and Large categories.

Table 4.8: Distribution of Sample Respondents according to Crop Production and Awareness Level

Crop production	Awareness level		Total
	High	Low	
No crop production	240(90.15)	20(9.85)	260(100)
Small	100(61.36)	72(31.65)	172(100)
Medium	100(78.14)	40(38.64)	140(100)
Large	80(41.26)	28(58.74)	108(100)
Total	440	160	600

Figure in paranthesis indicates percentage, D.F 2 χ^2 =6.9

As per the table 4.8 it is clear that in a sample of 600 respondents, 240 sample respondents were belonging from the category of No crop production, 100 sample respondents were belonging from small, 100 sample respondents were belonging from medium and 80 sample respondents were belonging from Large having low level of awareness.

To test the significance between age of the respondents and awareness level of the χ^2 test was applied. The calculation value (6.9) of chi-square is greater than table value (5.3) Hence, the hypothesis is not accepted. It can be concluded that there is no significant association between the Crop production and awareness level of the sample respondents about women agricultures and schemes.

CHAPTER V

SATISFACTION LEVEL OF WOMEN ENTREPRENEURS IN AGRICULTURAL SECTOR

5.1. Introduction

In the present study, by considering the importance and benefits of women entrepreneurs in agricultural sectors, an attempt is made to analysis the level of satisfaction about the women entrepreneurs in agricultural sector.

5.2. Qualifications of Data to Measure the Awareness Level of Women Entrepreneurs in Agricultural Sectors

A comprehensive interview schedule is design to collect the data from the sample respondents. Likert's type 5 point rating scale is applied.

To measure the satisfaction level about satisfaction, a list of 18 statements was given in interview schedule are prepared.

As per likert type 5 point rating scale ranges from 5,4,3,2 and 1 are used. It refers to 5 was Highly satisfied, 4 was Satisfied, 3 was neutral, 2 was Dissatisfied and 1 was Highly dissatisfied.

A total score for each responderts from all 18 statements are calculated by using the likert's 5 point rating scale technique. The maximum score of a respondents will be from all the 18 statements.

5.3. Measuring the Institutional and Schemes Awareness of Women Entrepreneurs in Agricultural Sector

In this present study, awareness about women entrepreneurs has been analyzed by giving 18 statements findings have been convert into score as per qualification procedure as stated in findings relating to institutions and schemes awareness are shown in a table.

H1: There is no significant relationship between socio economic characteristics (age, educational qualification, size of family, type of family, social particulars, land ownership pattern, crop production) of the sample respondents and satisfaction level of the sample respondents.

Table 5.1: Distribution of Sample Respondents according to Satisfaction Level of the Respondents

Satisfaction level	No. of the Respondents	Percentage
Satisfied	180	30
Dissatisfied	420	70
Total	600	100

Table 5.1 shows that the level of satisfaction of 180 sample respondents are satisfied in the agricultural sector, and 420 sample respondents are dissatisfied in the agricultural sector.

Association between Socio-Economical Characteristics of the Sample Respondents and Level of Satisfaction about Agriculture in Gobichettipalayam Town

It is expected that socio-economic characteristics of the sample respondents would influence the level of satisfaction about women entrepreneurs in agricultural sector. The following hypothesis has been framed on the basis of the review of the relevant studies and the outcome of the pilot study.

H1: There is no significant relationship between socio economic characteristics (age, educational qualification, size of family, type of family, social particulars, land ownership pattern, crop production) of the sample respondents and satisfaction level of the sample respondents.

5.3.1. Age and Satisfaction Level

Age is an important factor which may influence the agriculture womens. The present study is an attempt to relationship between age and satisfaction level. It is found that the sample respondents age ranges from 18 years to 50 years. In the present study, a sample respondents are grouped into young, middle and old categories.

Table 5.2: Distribution of Sample Respondents According to Age and Satisfaction Level

Age group	Satisfaction level		Total
	High	Low	
Young	148(94.31)	52(5.69)	200(100)
Middle	80(61.22)	68(38.78)	148(100)
Old	192(45.97)	60(54.03)	252(100)
Total	420	180	600

Figure in paranthesis indicates percentage, D.F 2 χ^2 =3.1

As per the table 5.2 it is clear that in a sample of 600 respondents, 148 sample respondents were belonging from the category of young age group, 80 sample respondents were belonging from middle age group, 192 percent of the respondents were belonging from old age group having low level of satisfaction.

To test the significance between age of the respondents and awareness level of the χ^2 test was applied. The calculation value (3.1) of chi-square is less than table value (4.8) Hence, the hypothesis is accepted. It can be concluded that there is no significant association between the age and satisfaction level of the sample respondents about women agricultures.

5.3.2. *Educational Qualification and Satisfaction Level*

Educational qualification is an important factor which may influence the agriculture womens. Education is a vital factor for the socio economic development. An education not only widens knowledge but also helps a person to make use of rational and scientific approach to solve problems. In rural areas, most of the farmers do not have the record up-to-date information on how to produce efficiently and economically. Therefore, it is expected that there may be a relationship between Educational level of the farmers and their level of satisfaction about the adoption of drip irrigation system in sugarcane cultivation. The present study is an attempt to relationship between educational qualification and awareness level. In the present study, a sample respondents are grouped into illiterate, school level, college level, professionals categories.

Table 5.3: Distribution of Sample Respondents according to Educational Qualification and Satisfaction Level

Educational Qualification	Satisfaction level		Total
	High	Low	
Illiterate	152(73.41)	64(6.59)	216(100)
School level	84(61.52)	40(38.48)	124(100)
College level	80(68.36)	32(31.64)	112 (100)
Professionals	104 (55.31)	44(44.69)	148 (100)
Total	420	180	600

Figure in paranthesis indicates percentage, D.F 2 χ^2 =6.1

As per the table 5.3 it is clear that in a sample of 600 respondents 152 sample respondents were belonging from the category of illiterate, 84 sample respondents were belonging from school level, 80 percent of the respondents were belonging from college level and 104 sample respondents were belonging from professionals having low level of satisfaction.

To test the significance between educational qualification of the satisfaction level of the χ^2 test was applied. The calculation value (6.1) of chi-square is greater than table value (6.7) Hence, the hypothesis is not accepted. It can be concluded that there is no significant association between the education qualification and satisfaction level of the sample respondents about women agricultures.

5.3.3. Nature of the Family and Satisfaction Level

Type of family is an important factor which may influence the agriculture women. The present study is an attempt to relationship between type of family and satisfaction level. It is found that the sample respondents families are converted into joint family and nuclear family.

Table 5.4: Distribution of Sample Respondents according to Nature of the and Satisfaction Level

Nature of family	Satisfaction Level		Total
	High	Low	
Joint	276 (79.94)	136(20.06)	412(100)
Nuclear	144 (39.46)	44(60.54)	188(100)
Total	420	180	600

Figure in paranthesis indicates percentage, D.F 2 χ^2 =4.4

As per the table 5.4 it is clear that in a sample of 600 respondents 276 sample respondents were belonging from joint family, 144 sample respondents were belonging from Nuclear family having low level of satisfaction.

To test the significance between age of the respondents and awareness level of the χ^2 test was applied. The calculation value (4.4) of chi-square is less than table value (5.01). Hence, the hypothesis is accepted. It can be concluded that there is no significant association between the nature of the family and satisfaction level of the sample respondents about women agricultures.

5.3.4. Size of Family and Satisfaction Level

Size of family is an important factor which may influence the agriculture women's. A family is defined as a group of persons, all related to each other. The number of members in it constitutes a family's size. If there is more number of members in the family, it is possible to do some activities which concerns about the agriculture. The size of the family reflects on the economic status of the farmers and this plays an important role in determining the viability of agricultures.

Number of members in the farmers' family ranged from 2 to 8.The present study is an attempt to relationship between size of family and satisfaction level. It is found that the sample respondents family sizes from the sample respondents are grouped into small, medium and large categories.

Table 5.5: Distribution of Sample Respondents According to Size of the Family and Satisfaction Level

Size of family	Satisfaction level		Total
	High	Low	
Small	144 (88.22)	84(11.78)	228(100)
Medium	244(69.92)	72(30.08)	316 (100)
Large	52(59.84)	24(40.16)	76 (100)
Total	420	180	600

Figure in paranthesis indicates percentage, D.F 2 χ^2 =5.2

As per the table 5.5 it is clear that in a sample of 600 respondents 144 were sample respondents belonging small, 244 sample respondents were belonging from medium and 52 were belonging from large families having low level of satisfaction. To test the significance between age of the respondents and awareness level of the χ^2 test was applied. The calculation value (5.2) of chi-square is greater than table value (5.84). Hence, the hypothesis is not accepted. It can be concluded that there is no significant association between the size of family and awareness level of the sample respondents about women agricultures and schemes.

5.3.5. *Social Particulars Satisfaction Level*

Social particulars is an important factor which may influence the agriculture women's. The present study is an attempt to relationship between social particulars and awareness level. It is found that the sample respondents are divided into no participants, participants and public leaders.

Table 5.6: Distribution of Sample Respondents according to Social Particulars and Satisfaction Level

Social particulars	Satisfaction Level		Total
	High	Low	
No participants	184 (74.6)	64 (25.4)	248(100)
participants	220(62.25)	44(37.75)	264(100)
Public leader	16(81.15)	72(18.85)	88(100)
Total	420	180	600

Figure in paranthesis indicates percentage, D.F 2 χ^2 =4.6

As per the table 5.6 it is clear that in a sample of 600 respondents, 184 sample respondents were belonging from the category of No participants, 220 sample respondents were belonging from participated and 16 sample respondents were belonging from public leaders having low level of satisfaction.

To test the significance between age of the respondents and awareness level of the χ^2 test was applied. The calculation value (4.6) of chi-square is less than table value (5.9). Hence, the hypothesis is accepted. It can be concluded that there is no significant association between the social particulars and level of satisfaction about the women agriculture entrepreneurs.

5.3.6. Land Ownership Pattern and Awareness Level

Land ownership pattern is an important factor which may influence the agriculture women's. The present study is an attempt to relationship between land ownership pattern and awareness level. In the present study, a sample respondents are grouped into No land, own land, Leased in and Leased out, middle and old categories.

Table 5.7: Distribution of Sample Respondents according to Land Ownership Pattern and Satisfaction Level

Land ownership	Satisfaction level		Total
	High	Low	
No land	144(79.6)	88(20.4)	232(100)
Own land	120(61.94)	80(38.06)	160(100)
Leased in	84(69.34)	32(30.66)	116(100)
Leased out	72(49.26)	20(50.74)	92(100)
Total	420	180	600

Figure in paranthesis indicates percentage, D.F 2 χ^2 =6.32

As per the table 5.7 it is clear that in a sample of 600 respondents 144 sample respondents were belonging from the category of No land, 120 sample respondents were belonging from Own land 84 percent of the respondents were belonging from Leased in and 72 sample respondents were belonging from Leased out having low level of satisfaction.

To test the significance between age of the respondents and satisfaction level of the χ^2 test was applied. The calculation value (6.32) of chi-square is greater than table value (6.7). Hence, the hypothesis is not accepted. It can be concluded that there is no significant association between land ownership and level of satisfaction about the women agriculture entrepreneurs.

5.3.7. Crop Production and Satisfaction Level

Crop production is an important factor which may influence the agriculture women's. The present study is an attempt to relationship between crop production and satisfaction level. In the present study, a sample respondents are grouped into No crop production, Small, Medium and Large categories.

Table 5.8: Distribution of Sample Respondents according to Crop Production and Satisfaction Level

Crop production	Satisfaction level		Total
	High	Low	
No crop production	204(71.54)	48(28.46)	252(100)
Small	124(60.32)	64(39.68)	188(100)
Medium	56(74.18)	40(25.82)	96(100)
Large	36(40 2)	28(59.8)	64(100)
Total	420	180	600

Figure in paranthesis indicates percentage, D.F 2 χ2 =5.8

As per the table 5.8 it is clear that in a sample of 600 respondents 204 sample respondents were belonging from the category of No crop production, 124 sample respondents were belonging from small, 56 sample respondents were belonging from medium and 36 sample respondents were belonging from Large having low level of satisfaction.

To test the significance between age of the respondents and satisfaction level of the χ^2 test was applied. The calculation value (5.6) of chi-square is less than table value (6.7). Hence, the hypothesis is accepted. It can be concluded that there is no significant association between the crop production and level of satisfaction about the women agriculture entrepreneurs.

CHAPTER VI

FINDINGS, SUGGESTIONS AND CONCLUSIONS

6.1. Introduction

Women entrepreneurs play an important role in all countries, especially in developing countries like India. The fifth round of National Sample Survey Organization (NSSO) in March 20002 defined "women entrepreneur as "an owned and controlled by women having a minimum financial investment of 51% of the capital and giving at least 51% of the employment generated in the enterprise to women". However, this definition is subject to criticism mainly on the condition of employing more than 50% women workers employed in the enterprises and owned and run by women. In a nutshell, women entrepreneurs are those women who think of a business enterprise, initiate it, organize and combine the factors of production, operate the enterprise and undertake risks and handle economic uncertainty included in running a business enterprise.

The basic objective of women entrepreneurs is the creation of employment opportunities. With the development of women entrepreneurs, there can be dispersal of industries in the country. Women entrepreneurs facilitate a more equitable distribution of the national income and they ensure the achievement of technical improvements. Since the labourers do not have any disturbance in their local and social habits and customs, women entrepreneurs lead to progressive improvement in productivity.

Objectives of the Study

In this present study the objectives may be followed by:

1. To assess the factors influencing the women entrepreneurs to enter into agricultural sector.
2. To examine the problems faced by the women agricultural entrepreneurs.
3. To identify the various rural women agricultural entrepreneurs schemes and their level of awareness about the schemes.
4. To measure the level of satisfaction of rural women agricultural entrepreneurs.
5. To determine the finding, suggestions and conclusions of the study.

Hypothesis

On the basis of the knowledge gained during the study and review of the various relevant studies the present study aim to test the following null hypotheses.

H0.There is no significant relationship between socio economic characteristics (age, educational qualification, nature of the family, size of the family, social particulars, land ownership pattern, crop production) of the sample respondents and their awareness level in schemes of rural women entrepreneurs.

H1.There is no significant relationship between socio economic characteristics (age, educational qualification, nature of the family, size of the family, social particulars, land ownership pattern, crop production) of the sample respondents and their level of satisfaction in agricultural sector.

Methodology and Sampling Design

The present study was conducted among agricultural women entrepreneurs in Gobichettipalayam town. A sample of 150 respondents has chosen for the present study based on sampling method. The primary data have been collected through survey method by direct personal interview with 150 sample respondents.

Universe of the present study is infinite. Hence, it is decided to use convenient sampling method. Originally it was planned and collected data from 180 sample respondents. Due to incompletion and non returning of respondents, it was possible to have been 150 sample respondents as final size.

Frame Work Analysis

In the present study it is decided to use various statistical tools like Garrett's Ranking and chi square test.

Summary of Findings

The present study is modest attempt to highlight t factors influencing, problems of women entrepreneurs awareness level and satisfaction level of women entrepreneurs in agricultural sector a study in Gobichettipalayam Town in Erode District. The findings of present work of summarized below.

H0.There is no significant relationship between socio economic characteristics (age, educational qualification, nature of the family, size of the family, social particulars, land ownership pattern, crop production) of the sample respondents and their awareness level in schemes of rural women entrepreneurs.

Factors Influencing Woman Entrepreneurs in Agricultural Sector

In this chapter an attempt is made factor influencing women to become an entrepreneurs in agriculture. The interview schedule method is adopted for the collection of require data from the sample respondents. The Garrett's ranking table used factor influencing by the sample respondents.

On the basis Garrett's ranking table, is found that the major factors to continue the family business with high mean score of 55.64 is proved to be the most important factor to motivate the factors influencing women entrepreneurs, self employment is mean score of 53.48 ranked as second, improved standard of living mean score of 53.32 ranked as third. And other factors followed by own interest, high profit factor, prestige in society, nearness to market, easy to start, prestige in society, to available the government loan, unique idea, technological knowledge.

Problems Faced by Woman Entrepreneurs in Agricultural Sector

In this chapter an attempt is made problems faced women to become an entrepreneurs in agriculture. The interview schedule method is adopted for the collection of require data from the sample respondents. The Garrett's ranking table used problems of the sample respondents.

On the basis Garrett's ranking table, is found that the major problems of the are problem of finance as indicated by its highest mean score value 53.27 this is followed by problem in marketing mean score of 50.12 is ranked as second, lack of education mean score value 50.65 is ranked as third. And other problems are followed by lack of awareness of government policies, no direct ownership of the property, health problems, irrigation/monsoon, lack of self confidents, male domination, discouragement from family members.

Awareness Level of Women Entrepreneurs in Agricultural Sectors

1.Age and Awareness Level

In the present study it is found that the table 4.2 it is clear that in a sample of 600 respondents, 100 sample responderts were belonging from the category of young age group, 160 sample respondents were belonging from middle age group and 180 sample respondents were belonging from old age group having low level of awareness. To test the significance between age of the respondents and awareness level of the χ^2 test was applied. The calculation value (4.6) of chi-square is less than table value (5.9). Hence the hypothesis is accepted. It can be concluded that there is no significant association between the age and awareness level of the sample respondents about women agricultures and schemes.

2. Educational Qualification and Awareness Level

In the present study it is found that table 4.3 it is clear that in a sample 600 respondents 200 sample respondents were belonging from illiterate,100 sample respondents were belonging from school level, 100 sample respondents were belonging from college level and 40 sample respondents were belonging from professionals having low level of awareness.

To test the significance between educational qualification of the and awareness level of the $\chi2$ test was applied. The calculation value (5.8) of chi-square is less than table value(6.1) Hence, the hypothesis is accepted. It can be concluded that there is no significant association between the education qualification and awareness level of the sample respondents about women agricultures and schemes.

3. Nature of Family and Awareness Level

In the present study it is found that table 4.4 it is clear that in a sample of 600 respondents, 256 sample respondents were belonging from joint family184 sample respondents were belonging from Nuclear family having low level of awareness.

To test the significance between age of the respondents and awareness level of the $\chi2$ test was applied. The calculation value (4.7) of chi-square is greater than table value (3.8).Hence, the hypothesis is not accepted. It can be concluded that there is no significant association between the nature of family and awareness level of the sample respondents about women agricultures and schemes.

4. Size of Family and Awareness Level

In the present study it is found that the table 4.5 it is clear that in a sample of 600 respondents 120 sample respondents were belonging small, 192 sample respondents were belonging from medium and 128 sample respondents were belonging from large families having low level of awareness. To test the significance between age of the respondents and awareness level of the $\chi2$ test was applied. The calculation value (5.4) of chi-square is greater than table value (4.01) Hence, the hypothesis is not accepted. It can be concluded that there is no significant association between the size of family and awareness level of the sample respondents about women agricultures and schemes.

5. Social Particulars and Awareness Level

In the present study it is found that the table 4.6 it is clear that in a sample of 600 respondents, 200 sample respondents were belonging from the category of No participants, 120 sample respondents were belonging from participated and 160 sample respondents were belonging from public leaders having low level of awareness.

To test the significance between age of the respondents and awareness level of the χ2 test was applied. The calculation value (6.3) of chi-square is less than table value(7.1) Hence, the hypothesis is accepted. It can be concluded that there is no significant association between the social particulars and awareness level of the sample respondents about women agricultures and schemes.

6. Land Ownership Pattern and Awareness Level

In the present study it is found that the table 4.7 it is clear that in a sample of 600 respondents, 200 sample respondents were belonging from the category of No participants, 120 sample respondents were belonging from participated and 160 sample respondents were belonging from public leaders having low level of awareness.

To test the significance between age of the respondents and awareness level of the χ2 test was applied. The calculation value (4.6) of chi-square is less than table value(5.1) Hence, the hypothesis is accepted. It can be concluded that there is no significant association between the land ownership and awareness level of the sample respondents about women agricultures and schemes.

7. Crop Production and Awareness Level

In the present study it is found that the table 4.8 it is clear that in a sample of 600 respondents, 200 sample respondents were belonging from the category of No land, 100 sample respondents were belonging from Own land, 100 sample respondents were belonging from Leased in and 40 percent were belonging from Leased out having low level of awareness.

To test the significance between age of the respondents and awareness level of the χ2 test was applied. The calculation value (6.9) of chi-square is greater than table value (5.3). Hence, the hypothesis is not accepted. It can be concluded that there is no significant association between the Crop production and awareness level of the sample respondents about women agricultures and schemes.

Satisfaction Level of Women Entrepreneurs in Agricultural Sector

1. Age and Satisfaction Level

In the present study it is found that the table 5.2 it is clear that in a sample of 600 respondents 152 sample respondents were belonging from the category of illiterate, 84 sample respondents were belonging from school level, 80 percent of the respondents were belonging from college level and 104 sample respondents were belonging from professionals having low level of satisfaction.

To test the significance between age of the respondents and awareness level of the χ2 test was applied. The calculation value (3.1) of chi-square is less than table value (4.8) Hence, the hypothesis is accepted. It can be concluded that there is no significant association between the age and satisfaction level of the sample respondents about women agricultures.

2. Educational Qualification and Satisfaction Level

In the present study it is found that the table 5.3 it is clear that in a sample of 600 respondents 276 sample respondents were belonging from joint family, 144 sample respondents were belonging from Nuclear family having low level of satisfaction.

To test the significance between educational qualification of the satisfaction level of the χ2 test was applied. The calculation value (6.1) of chi-square is greater than table value (6.7) Hence, the hypothesis is not accepted. It can be concluded that there is no significant association between the education qualification and satisfaction level of the sample respondents about women agricultures.

3. Nature of Family and Satisfaction Level

In the present study it is found that he table 5.4 it is clear that in a sample of 600 respondents 276 sample respondents were belonging from joint family, 144 sample respondents were belonging from Nuclear family having low level of satisfaction.

To test the significance between age of the respondents and awareness level of the χ2 test was applied. The calculation value (4.4) of chi-square is less than table value (5.01) Hence, the hypothesis is accepted. It can be concluded that there is no significant association between the nature of the family and satisfaction level of the sample respondents about women agricultures.

4. Size of Family and Satisfaction Level

In the present study it is found that the table 5.5 it is clear that in a sample of 600 respondents 144 were sample respondents belonging small, 244 sample respondents were belonging from medium and 52 were belonging from large families having low level of satisfaction. To test the significance between age of the respondents and awareness level of the χ2 test was applied. The calculation value (5.2) of chi-square is greater than table value (5.84) Hence, the hypothesis is not accepted. It can be concluded that there is no significant association between the size of family and awareness level of the sample respondents about women agricultures and schemes.

5. Social Particulars and Satisfaction Level

In the present study it is found that the table 5.6 it is clear that in a sample of 600 respondents, 184 sample respondents were belonging from the category of No participants, 220 sample respondents were belonging from participated and 16 sample respondents were belonging from public leaders having low level of satisfaction.

To test the significance between age of the respondents and awareness level of the $\chi2$ test was applied. The calculation value (4.6) of chi-square is less than table value (5.9) Hence, the hypothesis is accepted. It can be concluded that there is no significant association between the social particulars and level of satisfaction about the women agriculture entrepreneurs.

6. Land Ownership Pattern and Satisfaction Level

In the present study it is found that the table 5.7 it is clear that in a sample of 600 respondents 144 sample respondents were belonging from the category of No land, 120 sample respondents were belonging from Own land 84 percent of the respondents were belonging from Leased in and 72 sample respondents were belonging from Leased out having low level of satisfaction.

To test the significance between age of the respondents and satisfaction level of the $\chi2$ test was applied. The calculation value (6.32) of chi-square is greater than table value (6.7). Hence, the hypothesis is not accepted. It can be concluded that there is no significant association between land ownership and level of satisfaction about the women agriculture entrepreneurs.

7. Crop Production and Satisfaction Level

In the present study it is found that the table 5.8 it is clear that in a sample of 600 respondents 204 sample respondents were belonging from the category of No crop production, 124 sample respondents were belonging from small, 56 sample respondents were belonging from medium and 36 sample respondents were belonging from Large having low level of satisfaction.

To test the significance between age of the respondents and satisfaction level of the $\chi2$ test was applied. The calculation value (5.6) of chi-square is less than table value (6.7).

Hence, the hypothesis is accepted. It can be concluded that there is no significant association between the crop production and level of satisfaction about the women agriculture entrepreneurs.

6.2.   Suggestions

On the basis of the findings of the present study, the following suggestions are made.

- In the present study it is found that (wide table 3.1) 53.27 per cent of the women entrepreneurs are facing the problem of finance. Hence, it is suggested that the government should provide sufficient loans and subsides to the women entrepreneurs in agriculture, through commercial banks. This will lead to solve the financial problems faced by the women entrepreneur in agriculture.

- In the present study it is found that (wide table 3.1) 50.99 per cent of the women entrepreneurs in agriculture are facing problems in marketing. Hence, it is suggested that the government may take steps to start co operative societies especially for women entrepreneurs in agriculture sector to market their producers.

- In the present study it is found that (wide table 3.1) 50.65 per cent the women entrepreneurs in agriculture are faced lack of education. Hence, it is suggested that the government adequate vocational training to the community that enables them to understand the production process and production management. Government and non government agencies should tie up with the various educational institutions to assist in entrepreneurship development mainly to plan business projects.

- In the present study it is found that (wide table 3.1) 47.63 per cent of the women entrepreneurs are faced lack of awareness of government policies. Hence, it is suggested that the government should arrange number of many awareness programmes for the women entrepreneurs in agriculture. In order to increase their level of awareness in the various fields of their agricultural activities, through agricultural department and entrepreneurship development cell.

The majority of women entrepreneurs were feel risk in changes in organizational factors like expansion and diversification. The women entrepreneurs cell should come forward to motivate them and remove the frustration to shine in their business.

6.3.   Conclusion

Women are an important human resource of the nation and every state should try to utilize them as mediators of economic growth and development. Encouragement for women entrepreneurship is one of the ways for that. But unfortunately it is seen that the traditional mind set of the society and negligence of the state and respective authorities are important obstacles in the women entrepreneurship development in India. Apart from the responsibility of the state and society, absence of a definite agenda of life, absence of balance between family and career obligations of women, poor degree of financial freedom for women, absence of direct ownership of the property to women, paradox of entrepreneurial skill & finance in economically rich and poor women, no awareness about capacities, low ability to bear risks, problems of work with male workers, negligence by financial institutions, lack of self-confidence, lack of professional education, mobility constraints and lack of interaction with successful entrepreneurs are major problems of women entrepreneurship development in India. Therefore, there is need of continuous attempt to inspire, encourage, motivate and co-operate with women entrepreneurs, awareness programmes should be conducted on a mass scale with the intention of creating awareness among women about the various areas to conduct business.

References

[1]   Abdul Gani and Roshan Ara, Conflicting Works of Working Women : Findings of an Exploratory Study, The Indian Journal of Industrial Relations, Vol.46, No.1, Pp.61-87, 2010.

[2]   M. Abdullah, Women Entrepreneruship-A Case of Micro enterprises, New Delhi: Response Books, 2008.

[3]   S. Acharya, Strategic Entrepreneurial Development, The Utkal Business Review, Vol.XXIII, Pp.208-214, 2010-2011.

[4]   S. Advani, Designs on Scaling Up, Entrepreneur, Pp.38-40, 2011.

[5]   M.T. Akbar, Entrepreneurship education in Bangladesh : A Study Based on Program Inputs, South Asian Journal of Management, Vol.17, No.4, Pp.21-56, 2010.

[6]   H.F. Andreassi, Entrepreneurship:Opportunities and Challenges for Public Policy for the Low-Income Population, Journal of Management and Entrepreneurship, Pp.5-29, 2010.

[7]   S.T. Anil Kothari, Women Entreprenerus in Home Based Businesses : Issues and Challenges, Review of Professional Management, Vol.7, No.2, 2009.

[8]   M.S. Aroon Purie, Tapping Entrepreneurial Competitiveness. Business Today, Vol.18, No.16, 2009.

[9]   S. Ashok Kumar, Women Entrepreneurship in India, Regal Publications, New Delhi, 2009.

[10]   G.S. Azad, Development of Entrepreneurship among Indian Women : A Psychological Analysis, SEDME Vol.XVI, No.3, Pp.63-84, 1989.

[11]   G.S. Azad, Development of entrepreneurship among rural women, Entrepreneurship and Entrepreneurial Development, Pp.249-257, 1991-92.

[12]   Babu, Influencing Factors of MSMES-A Case Study of Chittoor District in Andhra Pradesh, Business Vision, Pp.35-40, 2012.

[13]   S. Bhargava, Developmental Aspects of Entrepreneurship, Response Books, New Delhi, 2007.

[14]   S. Bhattacharyya, Entrepreneurship and Innovation : How Leadership Style Makes the difference? Vikalpa, Vol.31, No.1, Pp.107-115, 2006.

[15]   K. Chandra, Entrepreneurial Success, Sterling Publishers Private Limited, New Delhi, 2006.

[16]   K. Chandran, Entrepreneurial Success-A Psychological Study, Sterling Publishers Private Limited, Hyderabad, 1978.

[17]   A. Chatterjee, Women in Panchayats: A Review, Yojana, Pp.24-27, 2011.

[18]   Dash, Entrepreneurship Development at the Village Level, Entrepreneurship and Entrepreneurial Development, Pp.269-283, 1991-92.

[19]   B. Desai, Fundamentals of Entrepreneurship, Swastik Publications, New Delhi, 2008.

[20]   Devika, Making Space for Feminist Social Critique in Contemporary Kerala, Economic and Political Weekly, Vol.XLI, No.15, 2006.

[21]   Dhameja, Women Entrepreneurs, Deep & Deep Publications Pvt.Ltd., New Delhi, 2004.

[22]   www.google.co.in

Empowerment of Rural Women Entrepreneurs in Agricultural Sector: A Study in Erode District of Tamil Nadu

Interview Schedule

Personal Details

1. Name   :

2. Age   :

a. 18-21   b. 21-25   c.25-30   d. above 30

3. Village   :

4. District   :

5. Education of Respondent

a. Illiterate   b. School level   c. College level   d. Professional

6.Nature of the family

a. Joint   b. Nuclear

7. Size of family

a.below 3   b. 3 to 5   c. 5 to 10

8. Occupation :

9. Social particulars

a. Non participation   b. Member of one organization

c. Member of more than one organization d. Public leader

10. Land ownership pattern

a. No land   b. Own Land   c. Land leased in   d. Land leased out

11. Credit procured in crop

a. No crop production   b. upto 50000   c. 50000-100000

d. More than 100000

Awareness about Institutions and Schemes

S.NO	NAME	AWARE	UNAWARE
1	Rural entrepreneurship development programmes (REDP)		
2	Integrated rural development programmen (IRDP)		
3	Development of women and children in rural areas		
4	Training of rural youth for self employment		
5	Support of training and employment programme		
6	Mahila Samriddhi Yojana		
7	Women's development corporation		
8	The National Policy for Empowerment of Women		
9	Norwegian Agency for Development		
10	The National Bank for Agriculturla and Rural Development (NABARD)		
11	Swarnajayanthi Gram Swarozgar (SGSY)		
12	Rajiv Gandhi National Creche Scheme		
13	TREAD subsidy schemes for women		
14	Prime Ministers Rozgar Yojana (PMRY)		
15	Indhira Mahila Yojana (IMY)		
16	Rashtirya Mahila Kosh (RMK)		
17	Krishi Vigyan Kendra (KVK)		
18	Tamil Nadu Corporation for Development of Women		

Factors that Influencing Women to Become Entrepreneurs

S.NO	FACTORS	RANK
1	Additional income for the family	
2	High profit factor	
3	To continue the family business	
4	To available the government loan	
5	To secure self employment / independent living	
6	Own interest	
7	Social status / prestige in society	
8	To improved standard of living	
9	Easy to start	
10	Unique idea / no competition	
11	Technological knowledge / training of present business line	
12	Nearness to market	

Satisfaction Level of Women Entrepreneurs in Agriculture

S.NO	SATISFACTION LEVEL	HS	S	N	DS	HDS
1	Commencing procedures					
2	Encouragement from family					
3	Location of business					
4	Availability of raw materials					
5	Price of raw material					
6	Availability of labour					
7	Efficient of labour					
8	Co-operation of labour					
9	Availability of loans from bank / financial institutions					
10	Availability of market					

Problems Faced by Women Entrepreneurs in Agriculture

S.NO	PROBLEMS	RANK
1	Lack of self confident	
2	Irrigation / Mon soon	
3	Discouragement of family members and others	
4	Problem of fiancé	
5	Male domination	
6	Lack of education	
7	Health problem	
8	Problems in marketing	
9	Lack of awareness of government policies	
10	No direct ownership of the property	

Any Other Information: